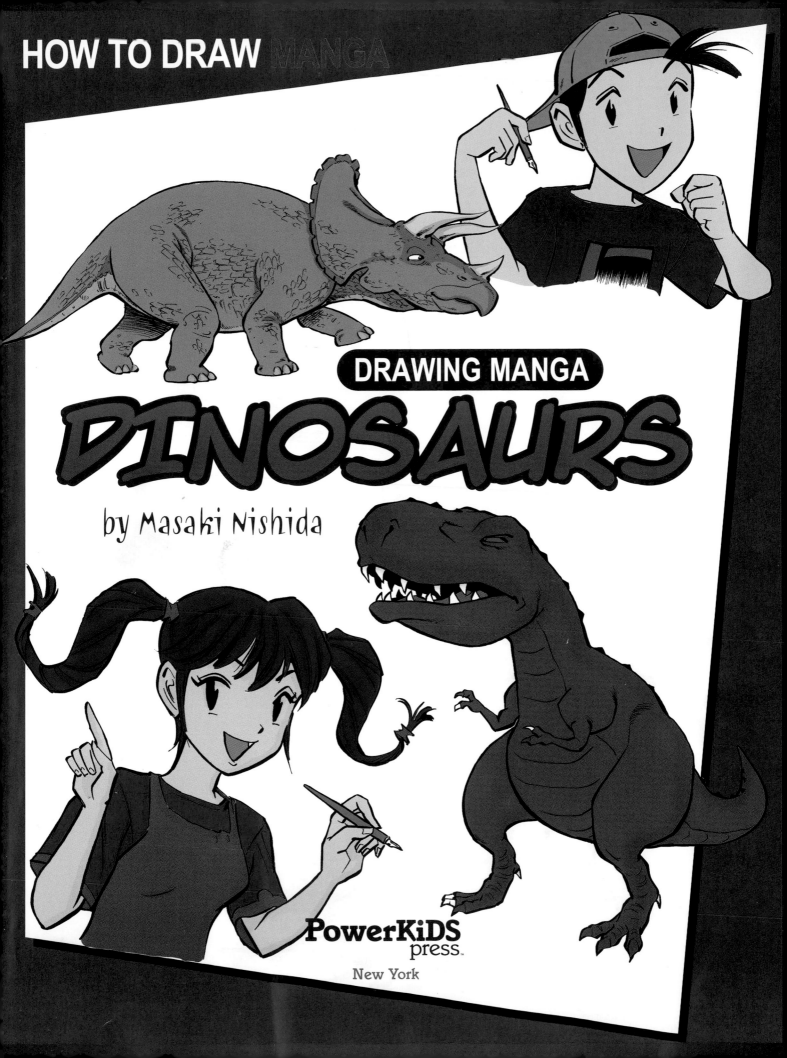

Published in 2008 by The Rosen Publishing Group, Inc.
29 East 21st Street, New York, NY 10010

First Edition

American Editor: Dean Galiano
Japanese Editorial: Ray Productions
Book Design: Erica Clendening
Coloring: Erica Clendening, Julio Gil, Thomas Somers

Manga: Masaki Nishida

Photo Credits: p. 23 (Tyrannosaur, Velociraptor, Oviraptor, Diplodocus, Stegosaurus, Triceratops, Pterosaur) © Joe Tucciarone; p. 23 (Elasmosaurus) © Chris Butler/Photo Researcher, Inc.

Library of Congress Cataloging-in-Publication Data

Nishida, Masaki, 1960-
  Drawing manga dinosaurs / Masaki Nishida.
     p. cm.   \ (How to draw manga)
  Includes index.
  ISBN-13: 978-1-4042-3845-9 (library binding)
  ISBN-10:1-4042-3845-X (library binding)
 1. Dinosaurs in art \Juvenile literature. 2. Comic books, strips,
etc. \Japan \Technique \Juvenile literature. 3.
Cartooning \Technique \Juvenile literature. I. Title. II. Series.

  NC1764.8.D56N57 2007
  741.5'1 \dc22

                                2006036866

Manufactured in the United States of America

CONTENTS

History of Manga

Hi! I am Masaki. I have always loved reading and drawing manga. Now that I am a manga artist, I draw many different things. I have created all sorts of drawings about history, sports, and adventure.

In this book my friend Sayomi and I will show you how to draw manga dinosaurs step-by-step. You can see her on the page to the right.

Manga has always been very popular among Japanese people. Manga is a **unique** Japanese art form that borrows ideas from American **comic books**, and also from American and European movies. Today manga has become popular all over the world. It is enjoyed by many people in many different countries.

The biggest **attraction** of manga is the combination of pictures and **text**. This makes it easy to follow the exciting **plots** of the stories. We can create all sorts of adventures using manga. In this book we will draw eight dinosaurs as manga characters. Come now, let's visit the manga dinosaur world!

The supplies you will need to draw manga dinosaurs are:
- A **sketch** pad (or a single sheet of paper)
- A pencil
- A pencil sharpener
- A ballpoint or a fine felt pen
- An eraser

Hi! My name is Sayomi. Masaki and I are going to help you draw manga dinosaurs!

This book will teach you how to draw manga dinosaurs. It will also show you how to **illustrate** a story using manga.

You can use your manga drawing skills to recreate these stories. You can also use these stories as **inspiration** to come up with your own stories and characters.

DRAWING A TYRANNOSAUR

Tyrannosaur was the most fearsome dinosaur of the Cretaceous period!

1 Draw an oval shape for the head.

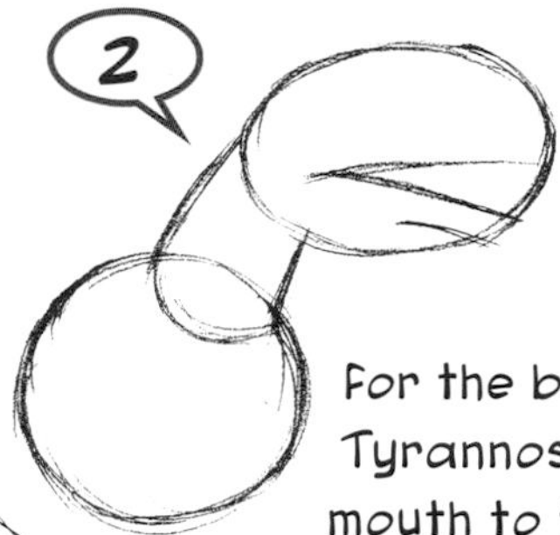

2 Add the neck and two more oval shapes for the body of Tyrannosaur. Add a mouth to the head as shown above.

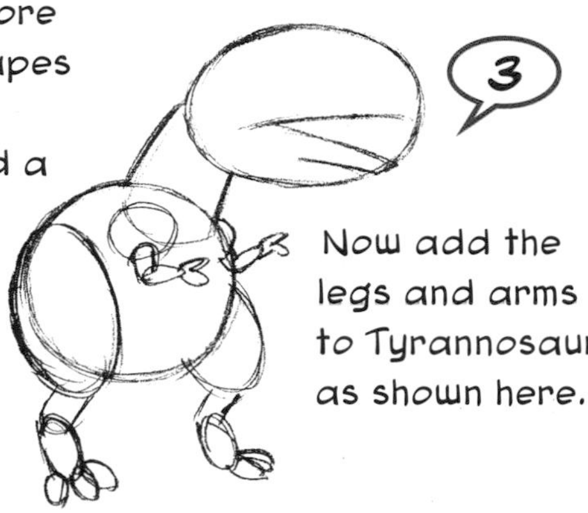

3 Now add the legs and arms to Tyrannosaur as shown here.

4 Add the eyes, teeth, tail, and other details.

5 Now we add ink to the drawing. Ink only the final lines you want to keep. Erase all pencil lines once ink is added.

6 Tyrannosaur is almost done! Finish the final details and shading. Color Tyrannosaur any way you like.

Read more about Tyrannosaur on page 23!

DRAWING A
VELOCIRAPTOR

Predatory dinosaurs eat other animals.

Velociraptor is a small predatory dinosaur.

1 Start with an oval shape for the head.

2 Now add lines for the neck and two ovals for the body.

3 Add the arms and legs, and draw the tail.

4 Now it's time to add details to the hands, feet, and head.

Detail of Claw

5 Ink the drawing and erase the pencil lines. Only add ink to the lines you will keep.

6 Add the final details and the shading. Color the velociraptor any way you like!

8

INTERVIEW WITH THE VELOCIRAPTOR

DRAWING A OVIRAPTOR

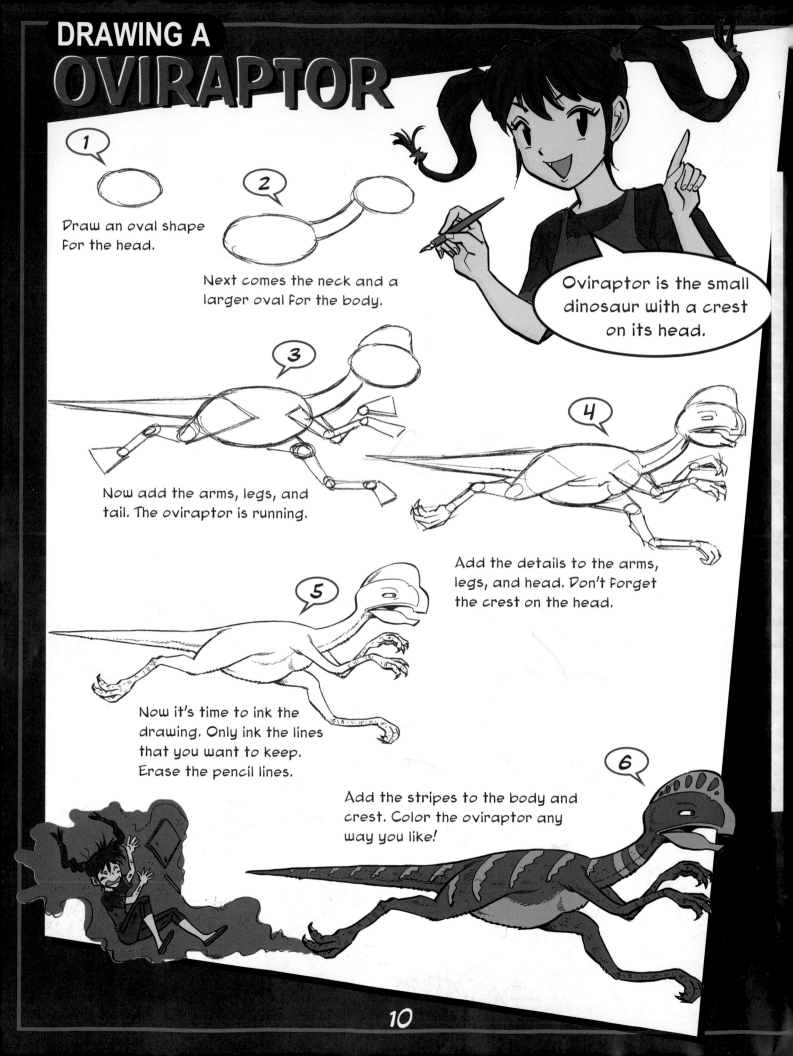

1 Draw an oval shape for the head.

2 Next comes the neck and a larger oval for the body.

Oviraptor is the small dinosaur with a crest on its head.

3 Now add the arms, legs, and tail. The oviraptor is running.

4 Add the details to the arms, legs, and head. Don't forget the crest on the head.

5 Now it's time to ink the drawing. Only ink the lines that you want to keep. Erase the pencil lines.

6 Add the stripes to the body and crest. Color the oviraptor any way you like!

OVIRAPTOR BASKETBALL

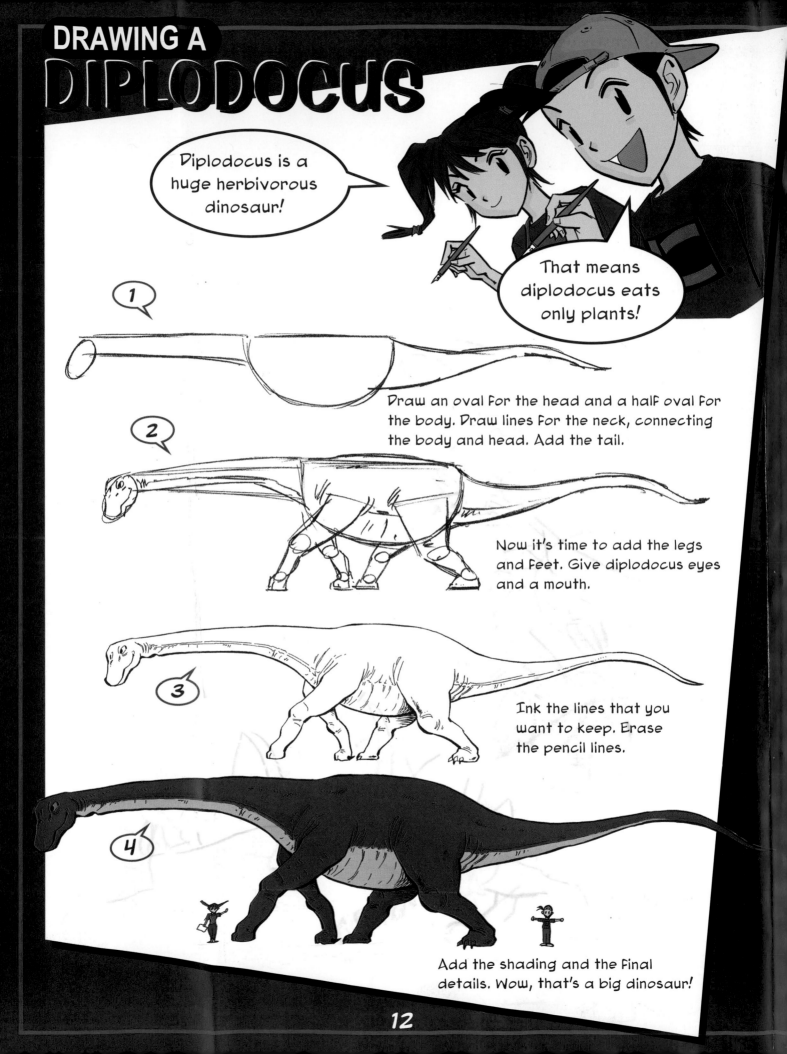

THE BIG TAIL

DRAWING A
STEGOSAURUS

Stegosaurus is an herbivorous dinosaur that has large spines on its back!

1 Draw a small oval for the head and a larger oval for the body. Add neck and tail.

2 Add the legs and the diamond-shaped spines.

3 Now add the eyes and the mouth.

4 Time to ink stegosaurus. Erase the pencil lines after inking.

5 Add the shading and the details. Add color if you like.

DRAWING A
TRICERATOPS

Triceratops is an herbivorous dinosaur with three horns.

Now let's draw!

1 Start with an oval for the head.

2 Now add a larger oval for the body and the neck.

3 Time to add the legs and tail. Draw a triangle above the neck and for the tail.

4 Now we add the face. Use three triangles for the horns on the head. Shape the legs, and add the ridges to the back of the head.

Time for the ink!

5

6 Erase the pencil lines and add details.

TRICERATOPS CIRCUS

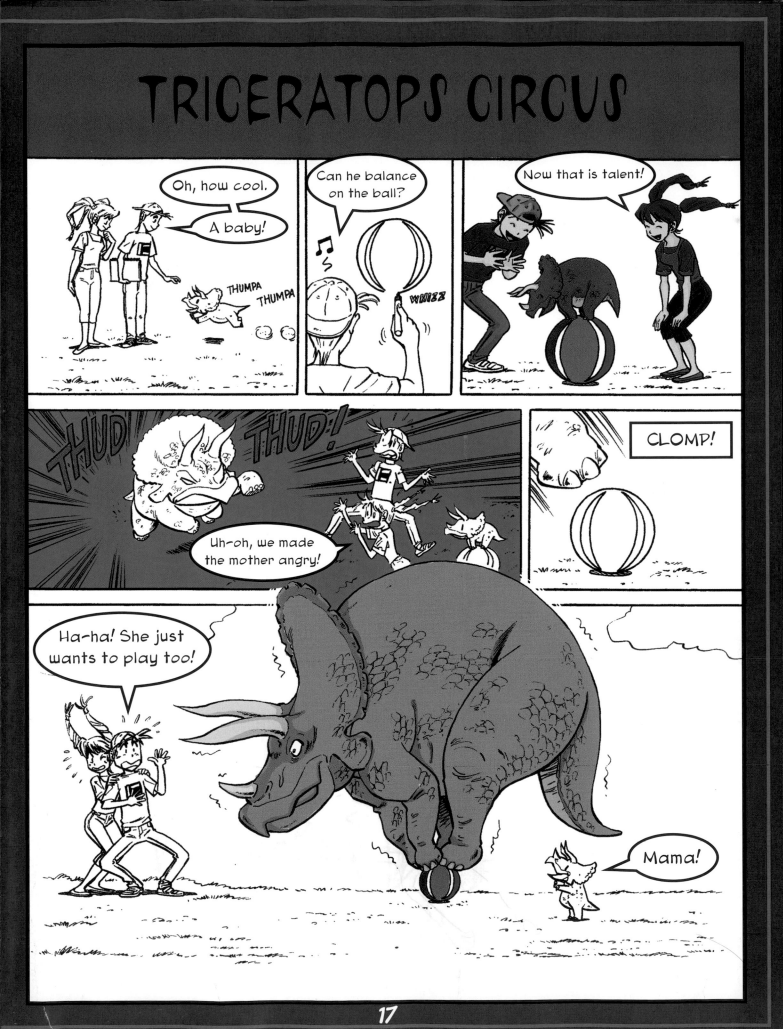

DRAWING A
PTEROSAUR

1

Start with an oval for the head and triangles for the beak.

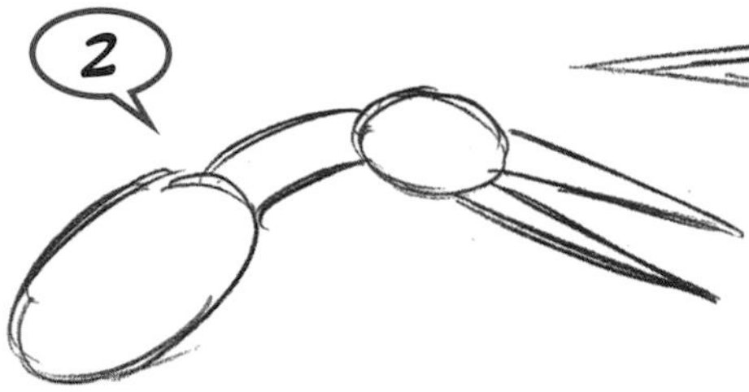

Pterosaur is a flying dinosaur.

2

Now add a bigger oval for the body. Connect the head and body with neck lines. Add the tail.

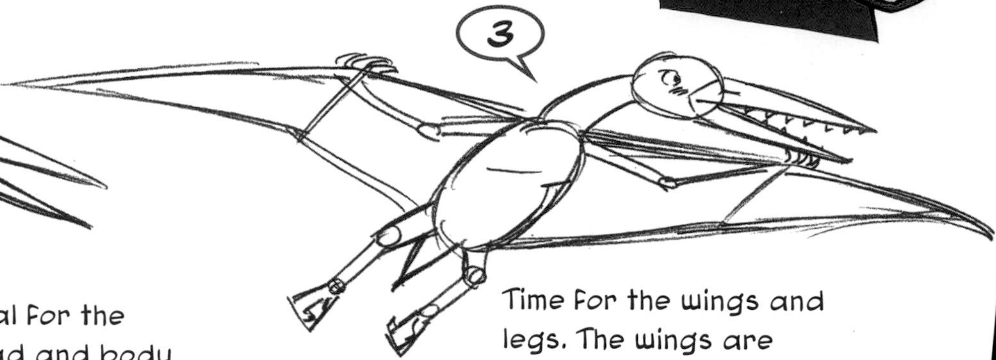

3

Time for the wings and legs. The wings are squares and triangles.

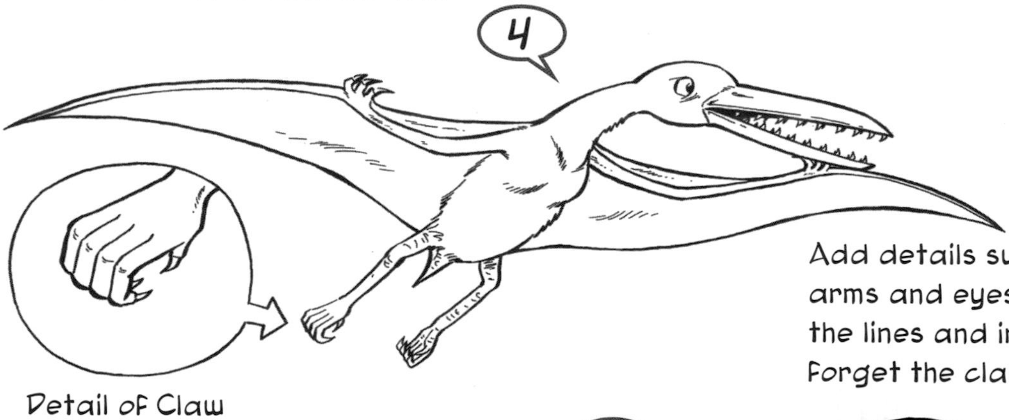

4

Detail of Claw

Add details such as arms and eyes. Clean up the lines and ink. Don't forget the claws!

5

That is one big bird!

THE PTEROSAUR RACE

DRAWING A ELASMOSAURUS

This dinosaur had fins and lived in the *ocean*!

1 Draw lines for the long, curvy neck. Add an oval for the head.

2 Now add a larger oval for the body and the fins and tail.

3 Shape the fins and add the face.

4 Now ink the lines you want to keep and erase the pencil lines.

5 Add the final details and color elasmosaurus any way you like!

GLOSSARY

admit (ed-MIT) To say something that is real or true.

atmosphere (AT-muh-sfeer) The character or the mood of a place.

attraction (uh-TRAK-shun) Pulling something together or toward something else.

comic books (KAH-mik BUKS) Magazines with cartoons that tell a story.

illustrate (IH-lus-trayt) To create pictures that help explain a story, poem, or book.

inspiration (in-spuh-RAY-shun) Where ideas come from.

plot (PLOT) The events that happen in a story.

request (rih-KWEST) Something that someone has asked for.

sketch (SKECH) A quick drawing.

temperature (TEM-pur-cher) The heat in a living body.

unique (yoo-NEEK) One of a kind.

yawn (YON) An opening of the mouth wide while taking a deep breath, often done while tired or bored.

Meet The Dinosaurs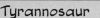

Tyrannosaur
Meaning: Tyrant lizard
Period: Upper Cretaceous
Length: Up to 12 meters (39 ft)
Diet: Carnivorous

Velociraptor
Meaning: Quick thief
Period: Upper Cretaceous
Length: Up to 1.8 meters (6 ft)
Diet: Carnivorous

Oviraptor
Meaning: Egg thief
Period: Upper Cretaceous
Length: Up to 2 meters (7 ft)
Diet: Omnivorous

Diplodocus
Meaning: Double beam
Period: Upper Jurassic
Length: Up to 26 meters (85 ft)
Diet: Herbivorous

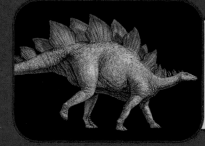

Stegosaurus
Meaning: Roof lizard
Period: Upper Jurassic
Length: Up to 9 meters (29. 5 ft)
Diet: Herbivorous

Triceratops
Meaning: Three-horned Face
Period: Upper Cretaceous
Length: Up to 9 meters (29.5 ft)
Diet: Herbivorous

Pterosaur
Meaning: Winged lizard
Period: Jurasic to Cretaceous
Length: Varies
Diet: Carnivorous

Elasmosaurus
Meaning: Thin-plated lizard
Period: Upper Cretaceous
Length: 14 meters (46 ft)
Diet: Carnivorous

INDEX